PLASTIC

Jewelry

LYNGERDA KELLEY & NANCY SCHIFFER

Revised & Expanded 4th Edition

Schiffer Publishing Ltd

4880 Lower Valley Road, Atglen, PA 19310 USA

Black Bakelite and brass pin. Red Bakelite
bracelet in shape of face. Red Bakelite and
brass pin jointed bracelet. Gold colored plastic
hair ornament. Silver and red Bakelite earrings.
(Bizarre Bazaar). Top: $125-150; $400-500,
Center: $250-300, Bottom: $40-50; $175-225

Revised price guide: 2001
Copyright © 1987, 1996 & 2001 by Lyngerda Kelley and Nancy Schiffer
Library of Congress Catalog Card Number: 00-109351

Typeset in Dutch801 XBdlt Bt/Dutch801 Rm BT

ISBN: 0-7643-1223-5
1 2 3 4

Contents

Acknowledgments 4
Evolution of Plastic Jewelry 5
Natural Plastics 10
Synthetic Plastics 16
Necklaces 28
Bracelets 42
Earrings 64
Pins and Clips 70
Rings 122
Groups 126
Buckles and Buttons 137
Bibliography .... inside back cover

The Dancing Sailor in Bakelite, 1940s. $125-150

Published by Schiffer Publishing Ltd.
4880 Lower Valley Road
Atglen, PA 19310
Phone: (610) 593-1777; Fax: (610) 593-2002
E-mail: Schifferbk@aol.com
Please visit our web site catalog at **www.schifferbooks.com**

In Europe, Schiffer books are distributed by Bushwood Books
6 Marksbury Avenue Kew Gardens
Surrey TW9 4JF England
Phone: 44 (0) 20-8392-8585; Fax: 44 (0) 20-8392-9876
E-mail: Bushwd@aol.com
Free postage in the UK. Europe: air mail at cost.

This book may be purchased from the publisher.
Include $3.95 for shipping. Please try your bookstore first.
We are always looking for people to write books on new and related subjects.
If you have an idea for a book please contact us at the Atglen, PA. address.
You may write for a free catalog.

Acknowledgments

The fun and novelty of wearing, collecting, or studying plastic jewelry easily becomes contagious. There is no end to design, style, color, or innovation. In our efforts to explore collectible plastic jewelry many people provided their ideas, sources, skills, as well as their collections, as the world of plastic jewelry rapidly grew. We are grateful to Marian R. Carroll, Dennis Cogdell, Frances Cronan and Frances Detweiler, Jackie Fleischmann, and Aggie Moore at the Black Angus Antique Mall, Adamstown, PA.; Ann's Arts in Chestnut Hill, PA.; Maureen McEvoy and Linda Morgan at the Islington Antique Mall, London; Rebecca Frey, Joan Leibowitz, and Lorraine Matt at The Lafayette Mill Antique Center, Lafayette, N.J.; Nora Lee at Bizarre Bazaar and Terry Rogers at The Manhattan Art and Antique Center, N.Y.C.; Bob Coyle and Marianne Ward at The People's Store, Lambertville, N.J.; Mim Klein in Philadelphia; Miss Genevieve and Kenneth J. Lane of Kenneth J. Lane, Inc., Patricia Funt, Michael Greenberg, Muriel Karasik, Angela Kramer, Carol Lupo at Trifari, Mark and Malvina Solomon and Fred Baekeland, N.Y. City; Ann Seeger and Robert Harding of the Smithsonian Institution, Washington, D.C.; Howard Aurbach and Ken Mafia of As Time Goes By in New Hope, P.A.; Karen Carmichael, Henry Chitwood, Wanda Johnson, Matilda D. Knowles II, Judy Pyle, Neal Davis, and Scott and Wendy Tyson.

Evolution of Plastic Jewelry

Colorful, lightweight and formerly inexpensive, plastic jewelry has been taken for granted in the past. But plastics have come of age. Now they are sought after as collectibles of skyrocketing value.

Bakelite, Lucite, and celluloid have become distinct names representing easily differentiated synthetic plastics found in jewelry over the last hundred years. The moldable property of plastics enabled this jewelry to be mass produced and originally inexpensive, yet of unique designs with many variations. Although molded, a great deal of hand-operated decoration has resulted in few identical pieces.

Many examples of colorful jewelry made from natural and synthetic plastics are presented in the following pages. The materials are explained, and a brief history of the styles will enable collectors to estimate dates of manufacture more readily. The manufacturers of plastic jewelry are for the most part unknown, since almost none of this jewelry was marked in any way until the most recent time.

The word "Plastic" comes from the Greek *Plastikos*: to mold or form. Plastic can be defined broadly as an inherently formless material which can be shaped under heat and pressure.

Molded black gutta percha pin, early example. (Jackie Fleischmann). $200-250

Plastic materials are divided into two groups, natural and synthetic. Natural plastics include amber, horn, tortoiseshell, and insect secretions that are used to make shellac. Gutta percha and rubber in its simplest form are among the synthetic plastics. Today the term "plastic" in its popular usage is taken to mean a synthetic material.

Jewelry has been made from natural plastics since ancient time. Amber, ivory and tortoiseshell have been shaped into beads for necklaces and used alone for bracelets, pins and hair ornaments, especially in the late nineteenth century.

In the second half of the nineteenth century, many scientific discoveries and industrial mechanization forever changed the products we use and our way of life. Advances in chemistry brought about the invention of cellulose plastic in 1867, casein plastic in 1897, and Bakelite resin plastic in 1907. These materials all were molded into countless useful products including jewelry.

In the early 1920s, when cast synthetic resins were found to be easy to work and color, jewelry manufacturers began experimenting with the new material to produce beads, molded pins and bangle bracelets. Wood, butterflies, and other materials were found able to be imbedded unharmed when the resin was cast around them. Mottled effects and pearlized finishes were gradually controlled in the 1920s. Therefore, inexpensive imitations of pearls were mass-produced from that time.

Bakelite trademark from 1939 Worlds Fair. "Molded on H-P-M Injection machine made by the Hydraulic Press Mfg. Co. Bakelite trademark registered U.S. Patent Office." (Karen Carmichael)

Synthetic plastics were highly successful in imitating the natural plastics like amber, horn, ivory, and tortoiseshell and continued to do so for many years. In 1919, celluloid jewelry was imported from Paris in a vast array of colors such as French blue, mottled green, yellow, white, purple and shell. These were made into pendants and ornaments strung on ribbon or as the links themselves. Galalith (a celluloid) was most popular in 1921 when it was frequently cut into different shapes or combined with metal for pins and necklaces. Then, with new designs of short sleeved gowns, bracelets were worn in profusion. Frequently both Bakelite and Galalith were set with rhinestones.

In the beginning, novelty plastic jewelry was purchased primarily by women looking for inexpensive colorful jewelry. However, it gained more universal appeal after 1925 when French clothing designer Co-Co Chanel introduced the idea of costume jewelry in her couture collections. Chanel also designed real jewelry which was often copied in plastic and other materials. It was not until the late 1930s that fashion magazines would recognize costume jewelry and even then there was very little discussion of plastic jewelry.

The Art Deco period, about 1925-1930 provided a boon to plastic jewelry with its geometrics, zigzag patterns and sleek style influences. Some French designers experimented with plastic, then, however they seldom signed their pieces. The workmanship found in plastic jewelry of this time is very good.

One person to know great success in the production of plastic jewelry in the 1920s in America was George F. Berkander. His company was located in Providence, Rhode Island which was, and is, one of the country's centers for the production of costume and novelty jewelry. Berkander began producing tortoise shell hair combs. In observing the rapidly changing styles in women's fashions, he progressed to bar pins which he eventually set with pearls and rhinestones and even some gold plated design elements.

Red Bakelite "Victory" pin with banner, c. 1940. (Wendy Tyson). $150-200

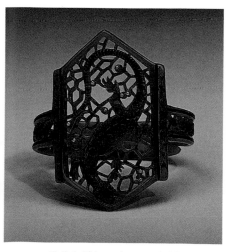

Celluloid bracelet, probably French, 1930s. $300-375

All of this he accomplished using plastic as his medium. By 1931 Berkander was making inexpensive bracelets at better than a thousand gross daily, using three tons of plastic materials a day. Berkander took credit for developing the first cellulose acetate flower pins, "celluloid elephant chains for the wives of Presidents Harding and Coolidge; and tiny celluloid airplanes with Lindbergh's name on them were ready for sale when the flyer landed in Paris in May, 1927." (Art Plastics, p. 43)

By the late 1920s Berkander had major competition from both New York and New England. Big producers of phenolic resin novelties such as Catalin and Marblette produced jewelry that was bold, colorful and very different from the more delicate celluloid designs. Much of Catalin and Marblette were made in more chunky designs as a result of the resins molding process.

In the making of jewelry, plastics were cast as rods, tubes, and slabs and then sliced into individual pieces or blanks to be formed and finished by the operator. Each worker completed a piece entirely on his own. Bracelets and rings were sawed from tubes and then carved by the individual operator. Floral and geometric designs were numerous yet each piece appears quite individual. The tedious hand finishing operation kept cast plastic jewelry in the higher brackets through the 1940s.

In 1929, the Depression hit the real jewelry market very hard. Plastic jewelry, however thrived for the next decade. It was reported that "40 to 50 percent of the jewelry sales in stores such as Saks, Bonwit's and Miriam Haskell were plastic." (Art Plastics, p. 41)

During the 1930s and 40s, manufacturers used thin sheets of celluloid plastic to make shaped jewelry forms. Dangles for bracelets and necklaces were cut out as flat shapes, then heated in hot water and curved. Hot needles could etch lines for further decoration, such as veins on leaves or scales and fur on fish and animal shapes. The shapes could also be embossed under pressure with machines specially designed for the job.

The practice of plating entire pieces of plastic was first attempted in 1910. It was, however, a fairly complicated electrolytic method and did not become wide spread until the 1940s. Even then it was very time-consuming and had yet to be perfected. Finally, in the 1950s, new techniques made it possible to plate plastics easily with a shiny metal surface.

In addition to plating, many plastics were set with plastic stones made to resemble precious gems. These pieces were higher priced designs but they also became popular. On the other hand, oversized, toy-like pins also were created in the 1940s. Many pieces of jewelry that were in imitation of real objects were made at least at life size, such as cherries. Figural pins of birds, animals, people and sports-related objects were made in large numbers. Chanel designed oversized translucent plastic eyeglasses and buttons both of which were studded with rhinestones. Plastic evening jewelry emerged in the form of larger, solid cuff bracelets set with stones and coupled with a matching belt buckle. The world renowned design house of Hermes experimented with plastic to create a bracelet watch decorated with black enamel and set into colored plastic, and a traveling watch. Cartier used acrylics for buckles on evening bags and other such minor embellishments. Elsa Schiaparelli began to use plastics in making jewelry and various trimmings in the late 1930s. One of her most notable plastic creations was a vinyl collar imbedded with multicolored metal insects featuring beetles and dragon flies. She also designed an ice cube necklace of pink crystal plastic cubes and unusual belt clasps, one having a pair of hands with painted fingernails. Pins of similar designs are shown on pages 87 and 114 of this book.

The war efforts of the 1940s included a jewelry collection promoted by Lord and Taylor to benefit Mme. Chiang Kai-shek's war orphans fund. Items such as gilt metal and plastic and replicas of Chinese jewelry were offered. In 1941, another wartime promotion took place in England. Lucky Bracelets were featured and sold for roughly one dollar each. They were made from the acrylic scraps used in the manufacture of bullet proof windscreens for Spitfire and Hurricane fighter planes.

The wartime shortages of all types of luxury goods turned many women toward costume jewelry. Glass from Czechoslovakia, which the costume jewelry industry had heavily depended upon was cut off to American manufacturers. Searching for substitutes for glass, various resins were found to be practical. Acrylics molded as gemstones or carved to resemble rock crystal were used as a substitute jewelry.

Following the war, the tendency in jewelry design was away from formal and geometric styles. "Plastic brooches and ear clips in contrasting tones, shown in colors such as cream and coral, or rose-pink and deeper red were popular, as were imitation Victorian cameos bearing a woman's head." (Art Plastics, p. 62)

The 1950s brought "Pop-It" beads. Each plastic molded bead had a type of plug end socket construction to it could all be attached to another bead to form bracelets and necklaces of varying lengths and combinations of colors. The beads varied also in size but not in shape and were soon relegated to the status of toys which were more fun to pop than to wear.

Much brightly colored plastic jewelry was manufactured in the 1960s. Clear Lucite beads and cast bracelets were embellished with rhinestones and metal confetti. The bright colors of this jewelry complemented the fashions designed for the young and fun-loving public. Plastic jewelry designs became more imaginative as they gained popularity.

By the 1970s, plastics were used to produce intricately molded settings and gem-like stones for use in other forms of costume jewelry including imitations of expensive, gem-set designs such as the copy of Jackie Onassas's necklace by Kenneth J. Lane.

The examples shown on the following sections display a wide variety of jewelry styles in plastic materials. Some are imitations of natural plastics and expensive gems, some are original forms, the results of designers experimenting with new materials. They are all beginning to take their places in the history of fashion design.

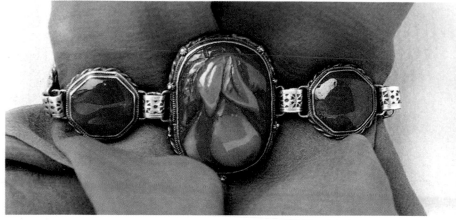

Amber link bracelet. Amber is soft and easily carved as has been done in this example. (Linda Morgan). $250-300

Amber necklaces. Both show variations in translucent qualities. The best quality amber is clear, but some are cloudy and some pieces show "stress marks" giving a crackled appearance. (Linda Morgan). $100-150 ea.

Natural Plastics

If it is understood that plastics are materials that can be softened, molded or pressed into a desired shape, it is apparent that there are numerous materials in nature which can be termed plastic. Natural plastics have been utilized in various ways by different civilizations.

Amber

Amber is a thermoplastic resin, meaning it can be heated, resoftened and remolded many times. Amber is a fossilized resin derived from trees that grew millions of years ago. The color ranges from a pale warm yellow to almost black.

Amber bead necklaces were popular in the early years of this century. To test for amber, heat a pin and insert it into an inconspicuous place on the article. The pin should go in easily. Professional non-destructive tests are recommended.

In the 1920s and 1930s, amber was widely imitated by less expensive synthetic plastics such as Bakelite and celluloid.

Victorian pin designed as rams head made of tortoiseshell. (Michael Greenberg). $300-400

Horn and Tortoiseshell

Horn and tortoiseshell are natural organic substances which have been made into jewelry since early times. Natural horn from animals, particularly Buffaloes, was ground, pressed into molds and heated to become a plastic dough. Boxes, buttons, ornamental pins and hair combs were molded in this way until the 1920s when horn was replaced for the most part by celluloid. Natural horn feels hollow and has a crackled, uneven surface. It smoulders when burned and smells like burned hair.

The shells of Hawkskill turtles were used to make small boxes, hair combs and jewelry particularly in the late nineteenth century. The mottled brown coloring of real tortoiseshell is caused by annual growth patterns.

Tortoiseshell has an irregular natural grain, burns with a flame and gives off an odor like burned hair.

Synthetic plastic imitations of tortoiseshell were among the early efforts of plastic manufacturers.

Gutta Percha

In 1843 Dr. Mongomerie, a Malayan surgeon found Maylay natives using the vegetable material gutta percha, a gum elastic, to make knife handles and other articles. It was a hard material that was scraped by hand from the Palaquium trees in Malaya, Borneo and Sumatra. Gutta percha was first softened in hot water and then pressed by hand into the desired shape.

Dr. Montgomerie's studies provided the impetus for the founding of the Gutta Percha Company in 1845, which remained in business until 1930. It was discovered that gutta percha had excellent electrical properties even when submerged in water and therefore, it soon became a major ocean cable insulation material. For a time, gutta percha was also used to make billiard balls.

Gutta percha jewelry can be found as bracelets, pins and earrings.

Papier-mâché and Wood Pulp

Papier mâché and pulp ware were used primarily for decorative purposes such as trays, tea caddies, and card cases which were very popular in the 1830s. One of the first pulp ware manufacturing companies was the Patent Pulp Manufacturing Company which began molding pulp ware in 1879 and continued until 1940.

Papier mâché is created by combining finely ground paper or wood pulp with animal glue or gum arabic and pressing it into a mold with reinforcing wire before drying. A more contemporary process was shaping layers of damp paper over a mold. Papier mâché jewelry was made as earrings, bangle bracelets, and pins. Due to the fragility of the material, few of these examples survive today. Papier mâché feels warm to the touch.

Vulcanite, Hard Rubber

Hard rubber which was the predecessor to vulcanite has been collected from the trees in Brazil for centuries. In 1820 it was discovered by Thomas Hancock that if rubber was cut up, heated and combined with a filler it could be molded into waterproof products. In 1839, as research continued, vulcanization was discovered. Rubber combined with sulfur creates a compound that is moldable and is unaffected by changes in temperature while at the same time, possessing a rubbery, resilient property. This discovery was made by Charles Goodyear who in effect had created the first commercially successful thermoset plastic.

Between 1861 and 1877, England's Queen Victoria permitted only black jewelry to be worn in her presence at court out of respectful mourning for her late husband Albert. This requirement set a fashion precedent which the English-speaking world followed. Black jet is an expensively-produced opal derivative mined in England from which black jewelry was made at this time. Alternatives were soon found in less expensive materials such as pressed horn, celluloid, casein and vulcanite. There are not many remaining examples of vulcanite jewelry but their place among early plastics must be noted.

Bois Durci

Bois Durci was a thermoset molding material patented in 1855 by Lepage in Paris. This compound was a blend of sawdust, blood, egg albumen or gelatin that was dried. Once it was compressed and heated, the substance became dark brown or black. Now very rare, Bois Durci moldings were common from 1860 to 1876. Lepage molded jewelry, combs, chess pieces and plaques.

Shellac

Shellac comes from the secretion of the *Croccus lacca* beetle found today in India and Malaya. The Egyptians used shellac to coat their mummies thousands of years ago. When shellac was mixed with fillers, it became a tough and moldable compound.

When shellac is pierced by a hat pin, it yields readily. When burned, shellac gives off a slight smell like sealing wax.

Shellac was first molded in the United States by Samuel Peck in the early 1850s to create "union cases." These became known as daguerreotype cases and were press-molded from a mixture of wood flour bound with shellac which gave the compound the ability to produce very fine detail.

In February of 1862, J. L. Baldwin obtained a U.S. Patent for his method of molding daguerreotype photo cases. His material was even called "plastic", even though its ingredients were of a mysterious concoction. Another patent, entitled "Compound for Picture Frames" called "for a material consisting of straw pulp mixed with one-half ounce of gum shellac, a quantity of alcohol to cut the gum, one-half ounce of glue, one-half pint of molasses, one-half pint of glycerine, and a quantity of ammoniacal solution of copper to make the pulp moist."

Daguerrotype cases were the most popular items produced in this kind of early plastic, but medallions, small boxes, soap containers, sewing kits, mirror backs and combs were also being made from it in the late 19th century.

Left: Two early bracelets in Victorian style, both using gutta percha. Delicate bracelet patented 1884. Bracelet with wide band and jet carved bouquet decoration in relief. (Ann's Arts). Top: $125-175, bottom: $350-400

Right: Two distinctly different hair combs. Black hair comb of gutta percha with chain links. Yellow horn comb with cut steel detail. (Patricia Funt). Left: $175-200, right: $195-245

Double chain of Celluloid oval links with pendant maple leaves of varicolored Celluloid amber tones, c. 1920s. (Smithsonian Institution). $200-250

Early example of necklace using gutta percha ornamentation in the form of black open circles surrounded and attached to one another with gilt metal, c. 1900. (Patricia Funt). $150-195

Gutta percha bracelets, both with wide bands and cameo style adornment. (Patricia Funt). $150-175 ea.

Synthetic Plastics

All plastics, no matter what their source, fall into one of two categories depending upon how they respond to heat. A plastic that can be repeatedly softened by heat and re-formed, like wax, is called a *thermoplastic*. This type retains its plastics qualities indefinitely. Natural plastics and cellulosics fall into this group. A plastic that once molded can never be re-softened or returned to a moldable state, like concrete is called a *thermoset*. Bakelite is an example of a thermoset plastic.

Collodian
The Swiss chemist Christian Schoenbine originally developed celluloid nitrate as early as the 1840s by combining wood or cotton fibers with nitric and sulfuric acids. This resulted in a highly flammable doughy material which was then used for explosives, called collodian. It did have, however, moldable properties that were of interest to other inventors.

Parkesene (Xylonite, Ivoride)
Alexander Parkes of England experimented with an early form of celluloid nitrate and developed a semi-synthetic plastic in 1855 which he called Parkesene. He had combined cotton fibers, or wood fibers, or wood flour, in nitric and sulphuric acids and had plasticized it using oils. Parkesene was eventually patented in 1867.

Parkes failed to make a commercial success of his Parkesene business and sold it to another Englishman Daniel Spill. Spill produced Parkesene in his own factory under the names of Xylonite and Ivoride. However, Spill was no more successful than Parkes had been and from 1865 to 1890 his business suffered continual setbacks.

Examples of Parkesene are cool to the touch, like ceramics.

Celluloid
The invention and practical production of celluloid was the first real synthetic milestone. At the same time that Parkes and Spill were experimenting with Parkesene in England, John Wesley Hyatt was working with a similar compound in Albany, New York. Inspired by the promise of a $10,000 prize for developing an inexpensive material to replace ivory for billiard balls, Hyatt experimented with cellulose nitrate and camphor heated under pressure. When cooled, his mixture became a solid block of clear plastic.

Although he did not receive the prize money he sought, Hyatt patented his material in 1869 and called it "Celluloid". In 1871 he formed

The American Celluloid Company and moved to Newark, New Jersey from where celluloid was marketed throughout the world. By 1880, celluloid was being manufactured in England and France. Eventually, Hyatt's company became the plastic's division of the Celanese Corporation.

Celluloid had wide applications industrially and in the photographic field. Specifically in jewelry, celluloid was made into hair combs, pins, bracelets and necklaces. It can be colored, made opaque, and etched, and these features all are found in the jewelry examples. Celluloid is extremely flammable and burns with the smell of camphor and nitric acid. It can be corroded by solvents and becomes soft when heated and brittle over time.

In 1920, a method was discovered to use a less-flammable variation of celluloid called cellulose acetate in injection molding processes creating the ability to produce many identical objects at the same time. This discovery helped to popularize plastic jewelry as its cost per item was brought down.

Cellulose acetate is known by several trade names, among them "plastacele" from the E. I. Dupont de Nemours Company of Wilmington, Delaware. A pamphlet published by this company in 1941 illustrates Plastacele jewelry in the forms of a necklace matching the one illustrated on page 17, of this book, bangle bracelets of elasticized links like those on pages 46 and 47, and a pin with dangling cherries like those on pages 75, 80 and 81.

Celluloid and its subsequent forms was made to imitate shell, ivory, coral, bone and hard rubber, tortoiseshell, amber, ebony, onyx and alabaster. It was commonly found in domestic settings as piano keys, napkin rings, camera film, pipe stems, combs, and toys as well as jewelry.

Casein

In 1897 casein plastics were first patented in Germany by W. Kriscke and Adolph Spittler who were looking for a material from which to make white "blackboards." It was manufactured in the United States in 1919. Today it is used primarily as a base for paint and glue. Casein was originally called Galalith from the Greek *gala*: milk and *litho*: stone. In England it was called Erinoid, allegedly because the milk used in the manufacturing process came from Ireland.

Natural casein is a protein found in milk which consists of long polymer molecules. The enzyme rennet taken from the stomach of an unweaned calf, is used to separate the natural casein from skim milk. The curd which settles from this reaction is dried, ground, purified and mixed with appropriate plasticizers and coloring dyes. This combination is then extruded into slots and rods, and hardened in a solution of water and formaldihyde. This new material is casein plastic.

Casein was introduced in Great Britain in 1913 as material for jewelry, knitting needles and crochet hooks.

Similar to celluloid in its visual properties, casein can be made in the same range of colors and patterns. Casein is found commonly as buttons, buckles, hair ornaments, gaming chips, dice, candlesticks and spoons. It can duplicate the natural materials horn, ivory, tortoiseshell and pearl. When heated, casein smells like burned milk or cheese.

18

Enlargement of salesman's sample showing Bakelite name and trademark. (Smithsonian Institution).

String of graduated oval facet-cut plastic beads of dark amber color, c. 1920s. (Smithsonian Institution). $175-250

Salesman's samples of Bakelite colors, c. 1920. (Smithsonian Institution)

Oppoosite page, bottom right:
Necklace and two medallions in Bakelite. Necklace on brown cord with translucent brown
medallion and imbedded design. Round translucent brown medallion. Six sided brown
translucent medallion pierced with two holes for hanging. (Smithsonian Institution). Top:
$95-125, BL: $115-135, BR: $125-150

Bakelite

Leo Hendrick Baekeland (1863-1944) was born in Ghent, Belguim, graduated from the University of Ghent in 1882 and entered the United States in 1889. Baekeland lived and worked in Yonkers, New York, where he had a small laboratory near his home.

Educated as a chemist, Baekeland discovered and produced Velox photographic printing paper which he eventually sold to Kodak Company in 1899, at the age of 37, earning three-quarters of a million dollars. With this fortune as a foundation, he found himself free to pursue independent research.

His reading of scientific journals brought to his attention the work of German chemists who reported a useless, hard material as a result of their work with phenol (carbolic acid) and formaldihyde. Baekeland began studying their experiments and working tirelessly in his laboratory, taking copious notes of all his efforts. Finally, he discovered a workable catalyst for phenol and formaldihyde and was the first person to realize that only under extreme heat and pressure would the resin polymerize as a thermoset.

Baekeland filed his famous patent in the United States on February 18, 1907. This was closely followed by his "Heat and Pressure" patent on July 13, 1907. He called his synthetic resin by the tradename Bakelite and registered the trademark throughout most of the industrial countries.

The substance Baekeland first produced was brittle and a pale amber color. It was not resistant to sun or oxygen and often turned dark. A filler of wood flour, cotton flock, asbestos or mica was added to increase the moldable qualities and add some pigment. These ingredients were combined with the resin and processed, a standard, dependable, uniform product emerged ready for shipment to custom molders.

Baekeland's research, as much as that of any other single individual, provided the foundation for modern polymer science. His studies were very complete and had significance beyond the commercial success of Bakelite. Baekeland's patent was in essence the birth certificate for a whole new industry and his research provided the text on which a whole new branch of science would emerge. Bakelite was not an inferior replacement for a natural material as many synthetics were, or a substitute for materials that were scarce or expensive. "It was superior in chemical, mechanical and physical properties." (J. H. Dubois, report to Plastics History Institute, c. 1950. p. 86, preserved in DuBois Collection, Archives Dept. Smithsonian Inst.)

Bakelite was first used commercially in 1910 and soon replaced amber, hard rubber and celluloid because it was both more economical and a superior substance for many uses. Primarily Bakelite found fame originally as an insulator for all kinds of electrical goods, and was used for machine parts that would withstand a great deal of friction.

In 1938, the Bakelite Company became the plastics division of the Union Carbide Company.

Baekeland used lead molds in the ovens with the heat hardenable resins.

In the molds the material was made into stock rods and shapes that lend themselves to being sliced off for bracelets and sold to fabricators. Baekeland maintained a monopoly on the compound until 1926 when the patent expired. Then companies such as Reichold began to produce Bakelite under the name of Catalin which was used to make costume jewelry.

In handling Bakelite it will be found to be warm to the touch, not cold or glossy. The colors were limited to dark shades of brown, red, blue or green. When mixed with other substances the colors can be expanded to include brown and black.

The molded color samples which Bakelite salesmen carried in the late 1920s are shown in the photograph on page 19. Bakelite has been successful in reproducing Jade, Carnelian, and Goldstone.

Bakelite is less than one-half the weight of glass, so the most decorative and large necklace can be worn with comfort. It has a refractive index excelled only by the diamond, and was understandably popular for use in jewelry. Bakelite acquires and retains a high lustrous polish because of its hardness and toughness. It is non-flammable and has no odor or taste.

About 1925, Bakelite pearls were found to be superior because they not only were indestructable and possess all the best features of other synthetic pearls, they were also light weight, warm to the touch and had a beautiful color and luster to them. They were made of a solid Bakelite base and retain their quality even today.

In the late 1920s Bakelite jewel quality was developed with a wider range of colors available, increased hardness, brilliance and luster which rivaled semi-precious jewels. It was also available in figured, cloudy

Price list and advertisement for Bakelite bracelets, c. 1924.

Bakelite Bracelets

A FEW popular styles of bracelets, some to match our necklaces, so that the much-in-demand matched sets of necklaces, eardrops and bracelets may be selected.

NO. B9 —A dainty chain mounted bracelet to match necklace B33 (see page 5) and furnished in the same colors ....ea. $1.50

NO. BR1—A lustrous circlet for the wrist, Amber, Cloudy Amber, Rose, Apple Green, Ruby, Sapphire, Jet, Violet ....doz. $7.20

NO. BR2—As above but larger, an arm bracelet.....................doz. $8.40

NO. BF1—Like BR1 but hand faceted in diamond cut ....doz. $10.80

NO. BF2—Like BF1 but arm size ....doz. $13.20

BEAD BRACELETS to match our round bead necklaces and available in all necklace shades. See page 9. Offered in three bead sizes as follows:

8 m/m ....ea. $1.80
10 m/m ....ea. $2.00
12 m/m ....ea. $2.20

Left: Necklace marked "K & L", probably German with three Bakelite ornaments on chrome links. (Karen Carmichael and Wendy Tyson). $195-235

Right: Plastic necklace of aqua and white beads in graduated sizes. Black and tan carved beads also graduated. (M. Klein). Aqua: $125-175, Black: $175-200

Plastic necklaces with variety of shaped beads. (Karen Carmichael and Wendy Tyson). $75-135 ea.

Two bakelite necklaces. Long beige, black and red drops on metal link chain. Black plastic links with yellow and black beads. (As Time Goes By). L-R: $295-350, $400-500

Yellow amber necklaces. The color of amber will vary widely from a pale yellow and honey to reddish-brown, brown, red and almost black. (Linda Morgan). L-R: $175-225; $225-275; $150-225

and shimmery iridescent effects. The new material was able to maintain its color and structure despite exposure to sun and the aging process.

In 1937 it was estimated by *Modern Plastics* magazine, that 5 1/2 million pounds of cast resin had been produced that year. About 40-45% was used in the manufacture of buttons and 7-9% in the making of costume jewelry. All genuine Bakelite was manufactured with a tag attached which bears the trademark 'Bakelite.' This tag was offered to licensed manufactures to insure the customer the authenticity of the material.

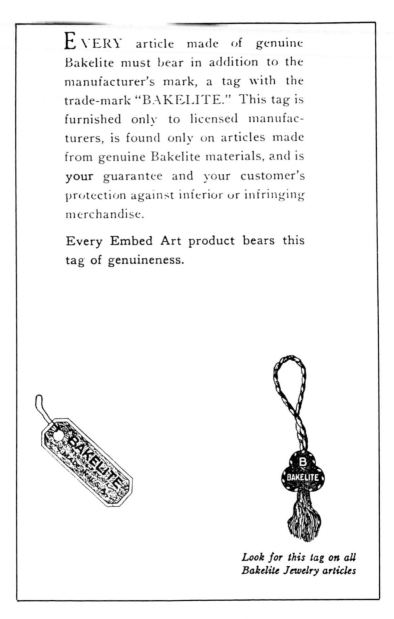

EVERY article made of genuine Bakelite must bear in addition to the manufacturer's mark, a tag with the trade-mark "BAKELITE." This tag is furnished only to licensed manufacturers, is found only on articles made from genuine Bakelite materials, and is **your** guarantee and your customer's protection against inferior or infringing merchandise.

Every Embed Art product bears this tag of genuineness.

Look for this tag on all Bakelite Jewelry articles

Embed Art Company's statement on Bakelite trademarks, 1924.

Acrylic Plastics *(Lucite)*

The original studies on acrylic plastics were done in Germany by Dr. Otto Rohn in 1901. By 1931 acrylics were being manufactured commercially as coating materials and safety bonding for glass. The acrylic plastics have crystal clarity, extreme colorability and valuable optical properties.

Two of the most well known acrylic resins are known today by their trade names Plexiglas and Lucite. They are thermoplastics and are among the most easily worked and polished. Acrylics are able to maintain their stability better than most other plastics.

An acrylic resin can be tinted any color or be used in a clear state. Acrylic jewelry was first designed and produced in Germany in the 1930s. Predominantly, these were faceted, engraved, molded and carved pieces like crystals.

It was reported in the May 16, 1941 *New York Times* that the patent for Lucite was given to Maximilian C. Meyer the president of Joseph H. Meyer Bros., a costume jewelry manufacturer in New York City.

The E. I. Dupont Company produced acrylic resins under the name of Lucite during World War II to make bomber nosecone and gun turrets.

Lucite has since been made into countless practical items for the home as well as beads and bracelets incorporating colored metallic pieces and rhinestones. Examples of rings, earrings and pins of Lucite appear in the following sections.

Bakelite necklace with brown beads of uniform size, c. 1920. Bakelite was made in round and faceted beads ranging in size from 6 1/2 to 20mm diameters. (Smithsonian Institution). $150-195

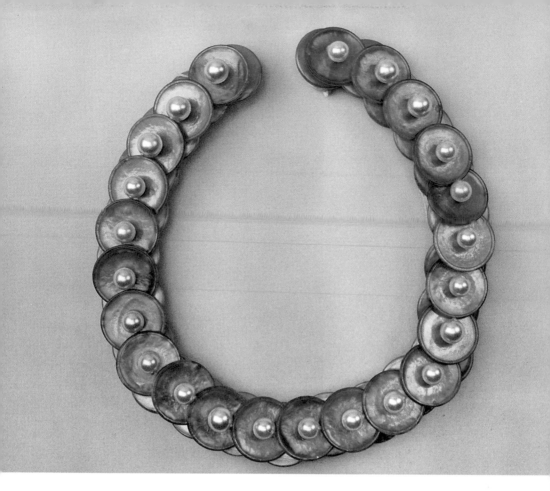

Button necklace made from turquoise plastic buttons with a pearl in the center of each. (Jackie Fleischmann). $75-100

Plastic Butterfly pin. Two plastic necklaces both alternating black beads with variously shaped with plastic chains. (As Time Goes By). Top: $50-75, center: $175-200, $150-175

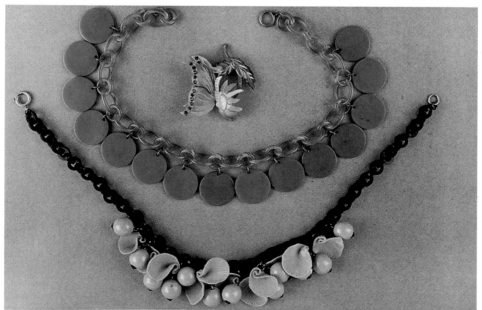

Alternating black beads with variously shaped and colored beads strung on black cord. Possibly Italian in origin, c. 1950. (Linda Morgan). $175-200

Plastic necklace in floral motif. Clear, green and white beads are used to design choker. (M. Klein). $50-75

Necklaces

Plastic link chain with plastic beads hanging from the links to form pendant style. (Jackie Fleischmann). $150-195

Advertisement for Bakelite pearls, 1924.

BAKELITE PEARL CHOKERS

Here are the Bakelite Pearl Chokers now so extremely popular. They need only to be displayed to be quickly. sold. Any woman will prize these lustrous pearls. They are very smart and effective, their dainty beauty having a distinct appeal—an unusual opportunity for increased sales and quick profits. Their superior quality assures lasting pleasure and satisfaction.

No. P-12—The medium or 12 m/m size bead............................Each, $6.00
No. P-125—As above but with alternating seed pearls.....................Each, 6.00
No. P-15—Large or 15 m/m size bead...................................Each, 7.00
No. P-155—As above but alternating seed pearls.........................Each, 7.00

All the above in any of the Bakelite Pearl colors or combinations of any two colors, alternating Pink and Rose or Primrose and Black pearls make particularly attractive combinations.

The clasps on all Bakelite Pearls are of sterling silver filigree, strongly made for durability as well as beauty. Many are set with finely cut stones—and identically fashioned clasps on the various items allow the selection of really "matched" costume sets.

Plastic "grey pearl" necklace strung on white thread. Grey plastic "pearl" bead on yellow metal straight pin, c. 1920s. (Smithsonian Institution)

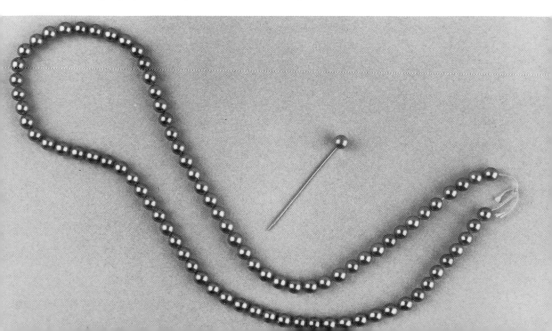

Bakelite necklaces in popular acorn and oak leaf design. One on clear plastic chain and one with brass chain. (As Time Goes By). $250-300 ea.

Clear Lucite necklace and earrings by *Castlecliff*. Red strawberry pendant necklace also Lucite. Bakelite jewelry box, c. 1930s. (Karen Carmichael and Wendy Tyson). Earrings: $200-250, necklace: $150-175, box: $200-250

Three red necklaces, two with matching plastic chains. Center necklace on metal chain. (As Time Goes By). Top to bottom: $325-375, $350-400, $275-325

Collage of Bakelite necklaces, assorted colors and types of design. Examples of beads in imitation of coral and jet as well as those utilizing the natural beauty of Bakelite itself. (Terry Rogers). Top to bottom: $195-245, $125-175, $135-185, $125-175, $195-250, $175-245

Example of advertisement for beaded necklaces made of Bakelite, 1924.

Reproduction of 1924 advertisement for Bakelite jewelry manufactured by the Embed Art Company.

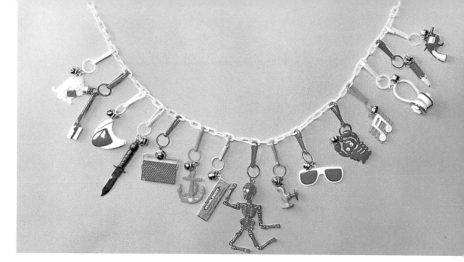

Contemporary plastic chain necklace, c. 1986. (Karen Carmichael). $50-75

Black plastic chain bracelet and necklace by Trifari. (Karen Carmichael). Set, $95-145

White plastic and brass link chain supports a bib of similar links with colored wooden beads. (M. Klein). $225-275

Plastic pierced drop necklace on plastic chain. Plastic amber colored fish pin. Purple and blue plastic flower pin. Oval backed pin with carved floral design. (Lorraine Matt). Top: $40-50, $50-75; center: $50-75; bottom: $100-150

Plastic and wood necklace. Multi-colored plastic chain holds groups of roughly squared wooden beads enhanced with small plastic beads and fastened with metal links and wire. (Karen Carmichael and Wendy Tyson). $225-275

Bakelite bracelet with gold colored chain and dark strawberries and leaves. Bakelite necklace with amber colored fruit and leaves, c. 1930s and 1940s. (Karen Carmichael and Wendy Tyson). Top: $175-225, bottom: $325-400

Bakelite necklace with clear link chain and amber and brown square beads. Green Bakelite bracelet with carved flowers and leaves. (Karen Carmichael and Wendy Tyson). L-R: $125-175, $175-225

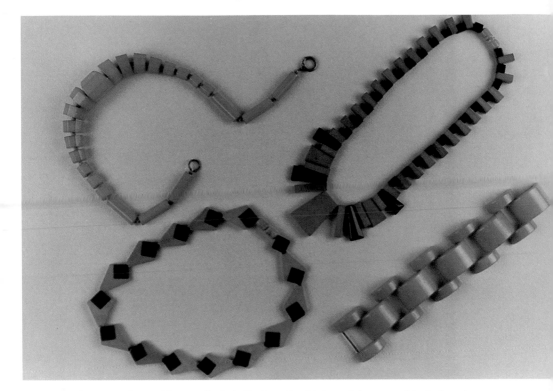

Three Bakelite necklaces and a Bakelite bracelet. Variety of shapes used in design of necklaces exemplify the versatility of Bakelite material. (As Time Goes By). Top: $200-250, $300-400; bottom: $250-325, $300-375

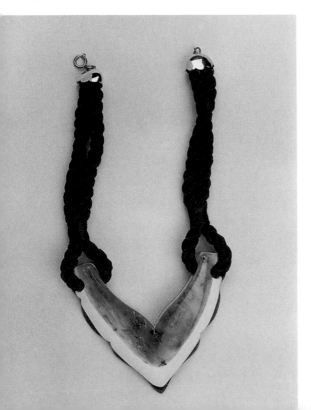

Bakelite necklace on brown cord. (Wendy Tyson). $200-250

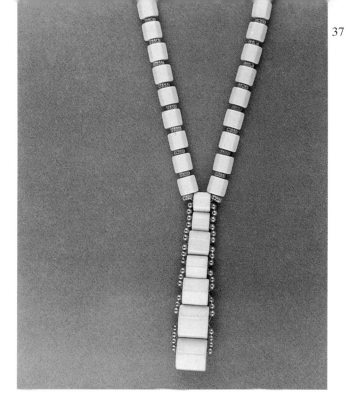

Bakelite ivory colored beads with gold spacers and graduated pendant. (M. Klein). $275-350

Designs in Bakelite and chrome from Germany. Matching light green bracelet and necklace. Chrome used in combination with dark green bakelite to create contemporary look. Bakelite colored to resemble ivory and enhanced with chrome beads and disks. (As Time Goes By). Matching set: $400-500, bottom left: $150-200, top: $150-225

Three plastic floral groups on silk woven cord to form choker. (M. Klein). $250-300

Assortment of Bakelite jewelry, all having the popular acorn and maple leaf theme. (Karen Carmichael and Wendy Tyson). Top right bracelet: $275-325, bottom bracelet: $350-400, remaining three (clockwise): $300-375, $125-175, $250-325

Celluloid pin and necklace in red leaf form. (Karen Carmichael and Wendy Tyson). L-R: $75-100, $100-150

Opposite page:
Necklace of black plastic
flowers each with rhinestone
center. Selected flowers
surrounded by rhinestones, c.
1970 by *Kenneth J. Lane.*
$400-500

Colorful layered plastic beads
of triangular shape, 1950s or
'60s. $40-75

Kenneth J. Lane's faux pearl and coral necklace with matching earrings and stick pin. The
imitation coral is of plastic, c. 1986. Set: $475-650

Bracelets

Translucent gold butterfly bracelet and black with green and gold marbling Bakelite bracelet. (Angela Kramer, Inc.). L-R: $500-750, $400-550

Bakelite belt buckle with gold toned face design. Four Bakelite bangle bracelets. Black bracelet has rhinestones set in as stars. Ivory colored bracelet has face design incised into the plastic. (Muriel Karasik). Buckle: $200-250, bracelets: $400-500 ea.

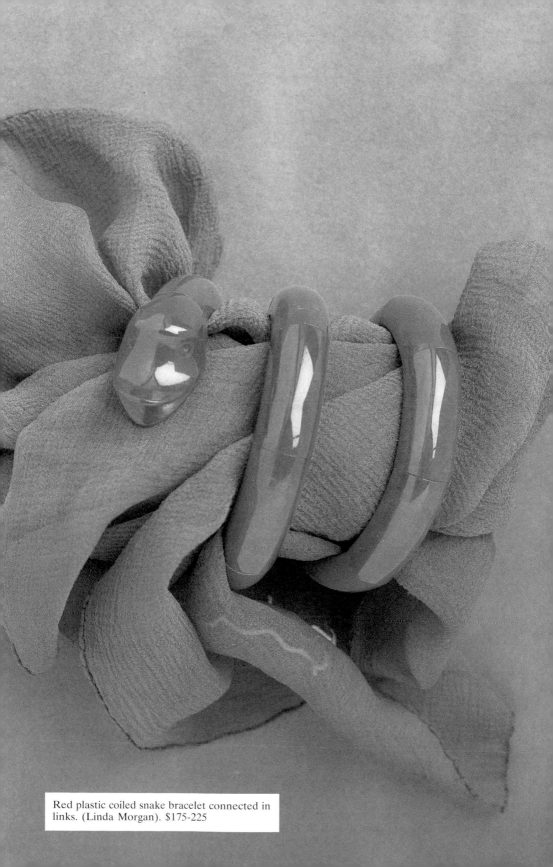

Red plastic coiled snake bracelet connected in links. (Linda Morgan). $175-225

Three bangle bracelets by *Monet,* "Directives," c. 1980. (Karen Carmichael). $45-75 ea.

Matching plastic bracelets to be worn above the elbow. Brown and cream tones in exotic design, c. 1930s. (Linda Morgan). Pair: $200-300

Plastic bangle bracelets. (Karen Carmichael and Wendy Tyson). Top: $500-750, $500-650. Bottom: $400-650, $600-750

Group of carved and decorated bangle bracelets. (As Time Goes By). $200-650 each (depending on complexity and detail)

Carved Bakelite bracelet, top and side view, c. 1920s. (Smithsonian Institution). $400-600

Ivory colored Bakelite bangles carved with decoration. (M. Klein). $75-250 ea.

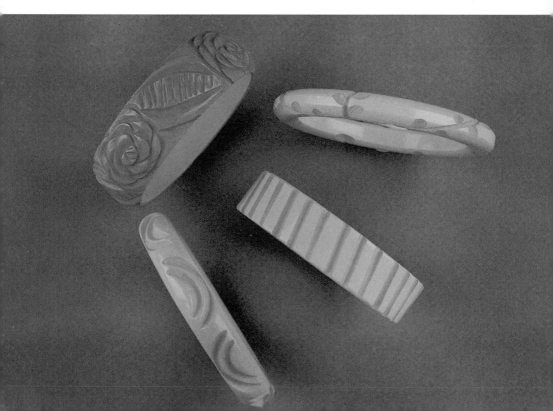

Three hinged Bakelite bracelets with cut work medallions. (Karen Carmichael and Wendy Tyson). T-B: $600-800, $300-400, $600-800

Group of amber toned Bakelite bangle bracelets. (As Time Goes By). $125-375 ea.

Carved and decorated Bakelite bangles all with hinged openings. (Karen Carmichael and Wendy Tyson). $225-375 ea.

Layered Bakelite bangle bracelets. (Karen Carmichael and Wendy Tyson). $200-350 ea.

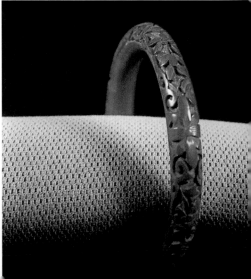

Chinese carved lacquer bangle bracelet. (Marian C. Carroll). $100-135

Plastic bangle bracelets. (Dennis Cogdell). $85-150 ea.

Varied plastic bangles.
(Franny's). $45-125 ea.

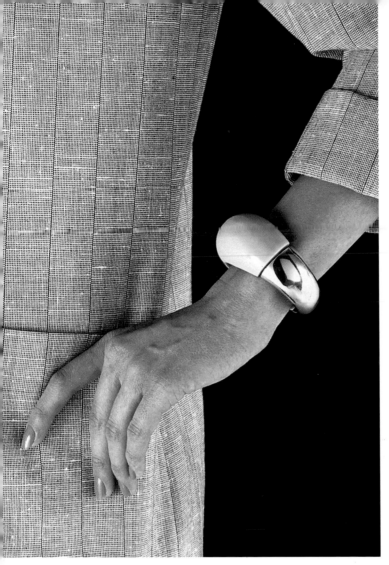

Trifari hinged bangle bracelet of plastic and chrome, c. 1975. $125-165

Two plastic bangle bracelets with contrasting color incised into the carved design by Diane von Furstenberg, circa 1980. (Karen Carmichael and Wendy Tyson). $125-150 ea.

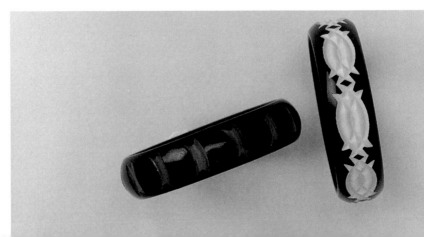

Group of Bakelite bracelets in variety of color, design, and
decoration. (Terry Rogers). $15-75 ea.

Four Bakelite bangle bracelets. (Wendy Tyson). $150-350 ea.

Group of Bakelite bracelets. (As Time Goes By). $125-275 ea.

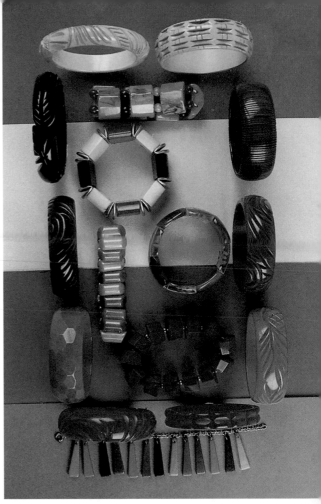

Yellow Bakelite bracelet with red polka dots, 1930s or '40s. $350-500

Group of Bakelite bangle bracelets. (Karen Carmichael and Wendy Tyson). $125-300 ea.

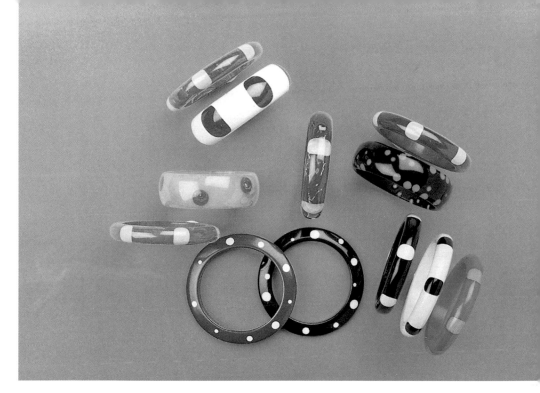

Polka dot Bakelite bangle bracelets. (Karen Carmichael and Wendy Tyson). $350-500 ea.

Bakelite bracelets. (As Time Goes By). $150-300 ea.

Bakelite bracelets. Two linked black bracelets with colored spots. Center yellow bracelet in style of Mah Jong pieces separated by black heads. (Muriel Karasik). L-R: $200-250, $125-175, $200-250

Pair of polka dot bangle bracelets. Black and white bangle decorated with rhinestones. Red linked bracelet. (Bizarre Bazaar). L-R: $250-300, $250-300 pr., $225-300

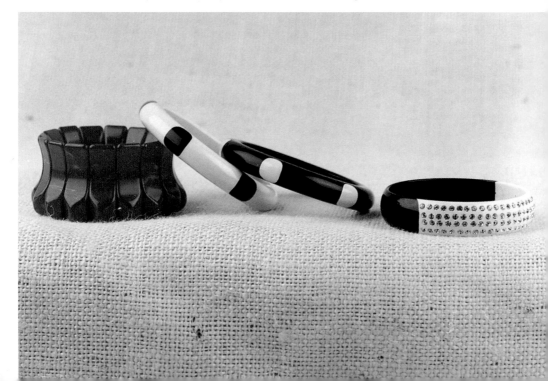

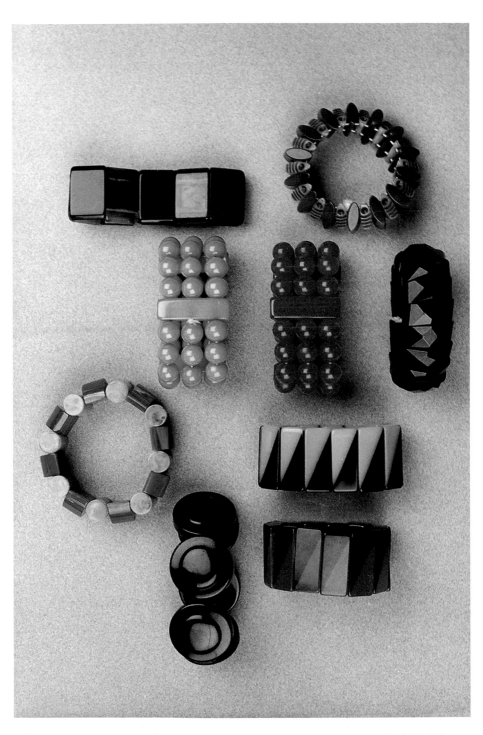

Variety of Bakelite and Lucite bracelets. (Karen Carmichael and Wendy Tyson). $275-375 ea.

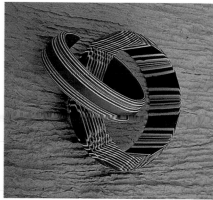

Clear plastic hinged bangle bracelet with glitter inside. (Ann's Arts). $125-175

Two layered plastic bracelets, red and white cuff and red, white and blue bangle probably made by Lea Stein, Paris, 1950s. $200-300

Three unique French plastic bracelets, probably made by Leah Stein. Multilayered links on elastic. Pastel facet cut links. Diagonal cut layered links, c. 1950. (Linda Morgan). $200-300 ea.

Red and white beads on elastic cord, form bracelet. Art Deco style European black plastic and chrome expansion bracelet. Four link cuff, signed *Sandra,* in yellow translucent plastic with brass nails. (M. Klein). Left: $75-100, Top: $175-225, Bottom: $200-250

Plastic necklace and bracelet with chrome decoration. Butterfly decorated bracelet and geometric hinged bracelet. (Linda Morgan). Necklace: $175-225, bracelets (clockwise): $3000+, $250-300, $175-225

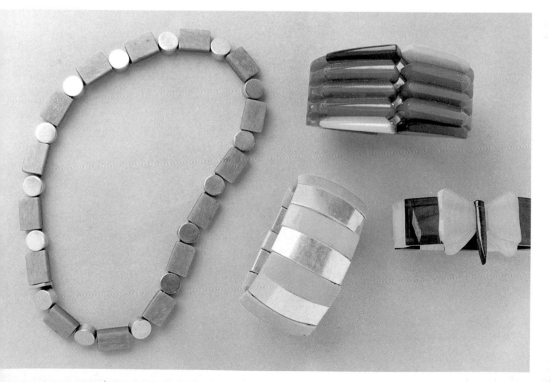

Bakelite bracelet of oak leaf and acorn charms on a metal chain. (Wendy Tyson). $200-250

Plastic and chrome link bracelet. Each square with an animal figure in chrome, left to right: alligator, frog, bird, elephant, rabbit, cat, monkey and dog. (Muriel Karasik). $250-300

Red, black and white Lucite bracelets. 1980s. (Karen Carmichael). $75-150 ea.

Four plastic decorated bangle bracelets. Two pair of earrings in dice style. Five rings with rhinestone decorations. (Karen Carmichael and Wendy Tyson). Rings: $85-135 ea., bracelets: $75-100 ea., earrings: $65-95 pr.

Group of Bakelite bangle bracelets, one with matching pair of earrings. (Karen Carmichael and Wendy Tyson). Green set: $125-150, bangles: $135-225 ea.

Aqua and ivory colored plastics. Aqua bangle bracelet made in Germany. Ivory look bangle bracelet marked *Napier*. (Karen Carmichael). Top: $40-50, $45-65, $40-50; bottom: $20-25 pr., $30-40 pr.

Opposite page:
Rhinestone decorated bangle bracelets and earrings. Pink and blue stone earrings marked *Weiss*. (Karen Carmichael). Sets: $275-350, bracelets: 150-200, earrings: $70-90 pr.

Earrings

Colored plastic flowers on clear plastic coated wire create earrings with tremblant effect. (Jackie Fleischmann). $75-125

Plastic earrings by Hobé enhanced with rhinestones and gold colored metal. (Jackie Fleischmann). $95-145

Two pair of plastic earrings in floral design complemented by rhinestones. (Jackie Fleischmann). $25-30 pr.

Three pair of molded plastic earrings show wide flexibility in plastic materials. (Karen Carmichael). Top to bottom: $45-65, $35-50, $40-60

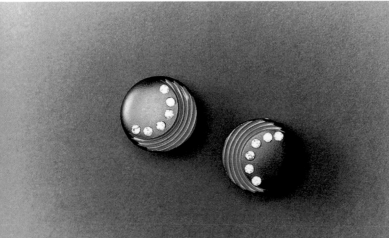

Group of Bakelite earrings in varying designs. (Terry Rogers). $25-50 pr.

Bakelite earrings in simple geometric patterns and shapes. (Karen Carmichael and Wendy Tyson). $25-125 pr.

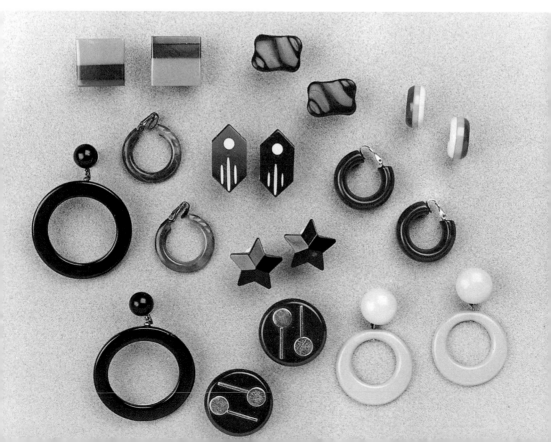

Plastic dangle earrings. (Jackie Fleischmann). $25-50 pr.

Pair of plastic earrings in image of donkeys carrying packs. Decorated with gilt enamel. (Jackie Fleischmann). $40-50

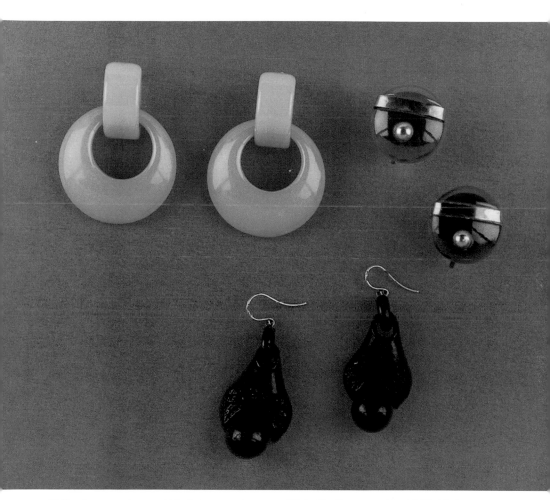

Yellow hoop earrings and black drop earrings are of Bakelite. Green earrings highlighted with metal are plastic. (M. Klein). Yellow: $40-50, black: $60-75, green: $30-40

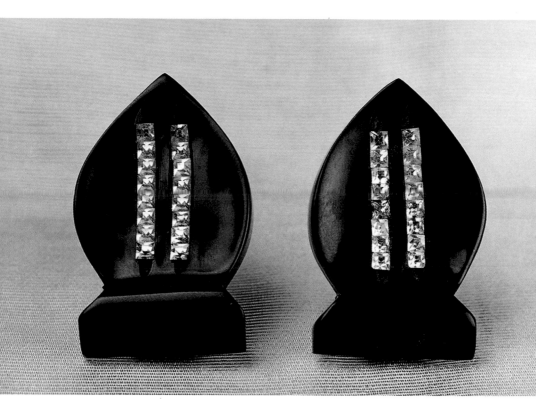

Black celluloid and rhinestone dress clips, c. 1920-1930. Celluloid was the first synthetic plastic, patented in 1869. (Dennis Cogdell). $95-125 pr.

Clock with Westclox movement in round plastic case. Black Bakelite pin with six red and one clear rhinestones on yellow metal background. Red Bakelite pin in leaf shape. (Ann's Arts). Pins: $65-75 ea., clock: $200-250

Pins and Clips

Casein and celluloid combined to form two unique dress clips, separated by brass insert, c. 1930. (Dennis Cogdell). $95-125

Oval carved Bakelite pin surrounded by metal chain along the edge. (Jackie Fleischmann). $95-125

Carved green plastic insert in brass pin setting, c. 1930. (Dennis Cogdell). $100-135

Modern plastic cameo applied to Lucite background, c. 1950-1960s. (Dennis Cogdell). $50-65

Casein pin with applied Celluloid in cameo style, c. 1930s. Casein introduced into jewelry making in 1919 to imitate tortoiseshell, pearl, amber and gold stone. (Dennis Cogdell). $85-125

Bakelite pin, set with rhinestones and painted black, c. 1930s. (Dennis Cogdell). $45-55

Black molded Bakelite pin with colored raised flower design. (Jackie Fleischmann). $85-115

Black glass crescent with beads. Clear Lucite base with etched design and black plastic diamond shape attached. Signed, *Weiss* shamrock pin. (Lorraine Matt). L-R: $35-50, $60-75, $50-65

Black medallion made to imitate black jet cameo. Appears to have hung from black Celluloid chain. (Dennis Cogdell). $95-135

Bakelite pin in black with oval drops attached with metal rings. (As Time Goes By). $200-250

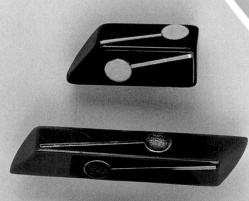

Transparent amber bar pin with plastic squares connected by metal and plastic links. (As Time Goes By). $185-235

Brown Bakelite pin with chrome lollipop decoration. Pair of black Bakelite dress clips also with same chrome lollipop motif. (As Time Goes By). Pin: $75-100, clips: $85-115

Laminated Bakelite in the form of three pins of different shapes and large bangle bracelet. (Karen Carmichael and Wendy Tyson). L-R: $750-1000, $300-350, $100-150 ea.

Amber colored plastic arrow pin with set rhinestones. Ivory colored Bakelite pin with rhinestone studded edge on two sides. (As Time Goes By). Top: $125-150, bottom: $145-175

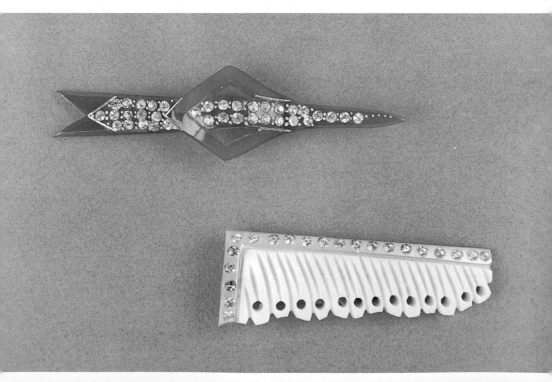

Amber faceted pin of floral design combining opaque and transparent shades of amber. (Linda Morgan). $125-150

Yellow and red celluloid flowers with rhinestone enhancement. (Becky Frey). $70-90 ea.

Bakelite floral motif pin. Multicolored enhanced with set rhinestones, c. 1940. (Dennis Cogdell). $200-250

Early style Lucite of molded flowers inside clear setting with opaque background. (Dennis Cogdell). $45-65

Plastic pins combining color, design, shape and materials. (Linda Morgan). Left: $150-175 ea., right: $125-150

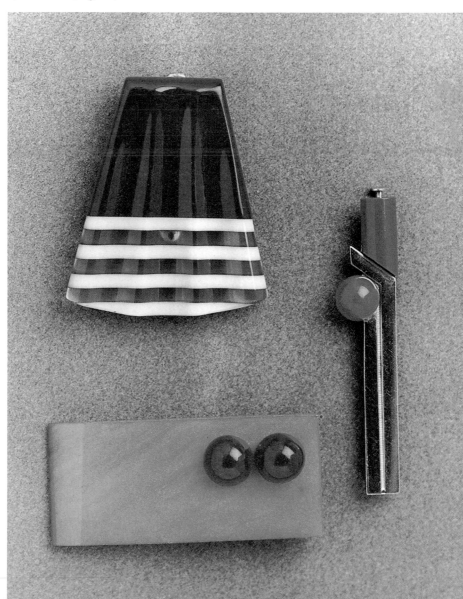

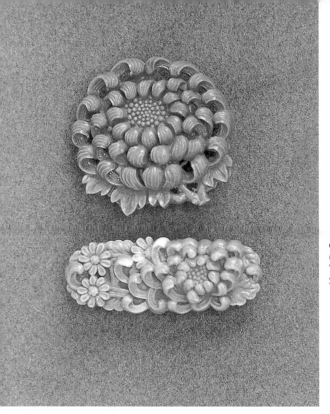

Opposite page: Group of Celluloid pins. Chrysanthemum and basket of flowers pins are marked, Japan. (Mark Solomon). Top to bottom: $35-45, $50-60 ea., $48-65, $55-70

Two Celluloid pins in imitation of coral. Floral incised decoration. (Karen Carmichael and Wendy Tyson). Top: $40-50, bottom: $35-45

Green Bakelite flower with leaves in lighter shade. Brown floral design Bakelite dress clips. Pair of Bakelite earrings in shape of flowers with colored rhinestones. White Bakelite dress clip also in floral motif with dark blue alternating petals and edged leaves. (Terry Rogers). Top: $75-100, $85-115, pr., bottom: $25-35, $30-40

Assorted styles of Bakelite pins. (As Time Goes By). Top: $95-115, $95-115, $225-275, center: $200-250, $125-150, $150-200, bottom: $200-250, $300-350, $125-175

Group of Bakelite carved flowers, pins and clips. (Karen Carmichael and Wendy Tyson). Clockwise: $90-140, $125-175 pr., $95-110, $90-110, $90-110, $125-175 pr., $175-225; center: $200-250

Group of Bakelite pins and two pair of earrings in ever popular floral theme. (Karen Carmichael and Wendy Tyson). Pins, $250-400 ea., earrings: $50-75 pr.

Opposite page:
Bakelite fruit pins. (Karen Carmichael and
Wendy Tyson). Clockwise (starting w/banana):
$275-325, $250-300, $275-325, $275-325,
$250-300, $250-300, $200-225, $225-275 ea.;
center: $450-550

Lucite pins, clear with painted backgrounds. Turtle pin is in wooden frame. (Wanda Johnson and Karen Carmichael). Top: $150-175, $125-160, $175-200; center: $135-155, $175-200, $150-175; bottom: $200-250, $185-225, $200-225

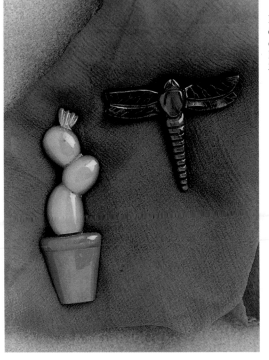

Lucite pin with yellow stems and clear petals tied together with clear Lucite ribbon. Orange plastic leaf clip. Small pin of three plastic limes. Lucite lily with green leaf, orange pistil and white petal. (M. Klein). L-R: $150-175, $95-145, $95-135, $125-150

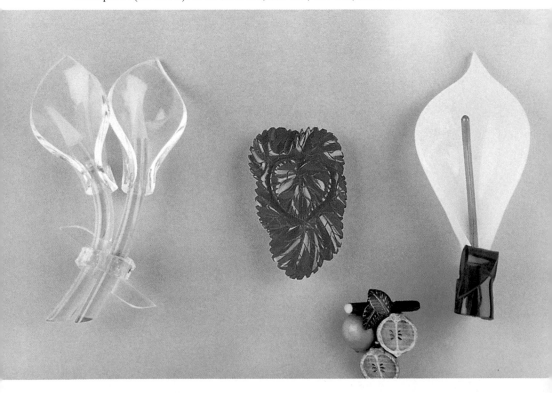

Group of Celluloid pins in variety of forms. (Karen Carmichael and Wendy Tyson). Left picture (in columns): 1st column: $100-145, 2nd: $125-150pr., $100-125, 3rd: $110-135, $100-130, $150-175. Right picture: 1st column: $125-150, $110-140, 2nd: $95-115, $115-135, $75-100, 3rd: $95-110

Bakelite pins in forms of potted plant and a palm tree. (Karen Carmichael and Wendy Tyson). L-R: $200-250, $300-375

Two pears together in Bakelite buckle. (Wendy Tyson). $300-350

Opposite page:
Matching set of necklace and bracelet made in
Bakelite. Necklace with red plastic chain and
pendant of fruit on brown background. Red links
form to make the bracelet with matching
medallion attached. (Karen Carmichael and
Wendy Tyson). L-R: $375-400, $475+

Popular Bakelite cherries in necklaces, pins and bracelets. All on plastic chains using metal links to attach cherries and leaves. (Karen Carmichael and Wendy Tyson). Top: $300-350, $375-425, $475+; bottom: $325-375, $350-375, $200-250, $225-275, $200-275

Grouping of Bakelite
cherry pins in various
styles: hearts, bows,
bar pins, and leaves.
(As Time Goes By).
Clockwise: $275-325,
$325-375, $150-185,
$150-200, $185-225;
center: $325-375

Red and black
Bakelite bows, one
with dangling cherries.
(Karen Carmichael).
Top: $125-150,
bottom: $185-245

Three Bakelite heart pins, two using cherry motif. (Karen Carmichael). L-R: $275-325, $375-450, $275-375

More Bakelite cherries, pins and earrings, c. 1930-1940. (Karen Carmichael and Wendy Tyson). Top: $150-185, $175-200, $275-325, center: $275-325, bottom: $65-85, $150-175

Assorted designs of Bakelite pins and heart pendant necklace. (Wanda Johnson). Clockwise (starting w/pineapple): $35-50, $115-135, $70-95, $150-195, $85-115, $200-250, $95-115 pr., $135-175, $140-185; center: $100-125(beads), $40-55(star)

Bakelite pin and earrings in style of hats, c. 1930-1940. (Karen Carmichael and Wendy Tyson). L-R: $100-125 pr., $375-500

Pins combining plastic and Bakelite materials. (As Time Goes By). Top: $75-100; center: $95-125, $300-350, $95-145; bottom: $250-275, $175-200, $125-175

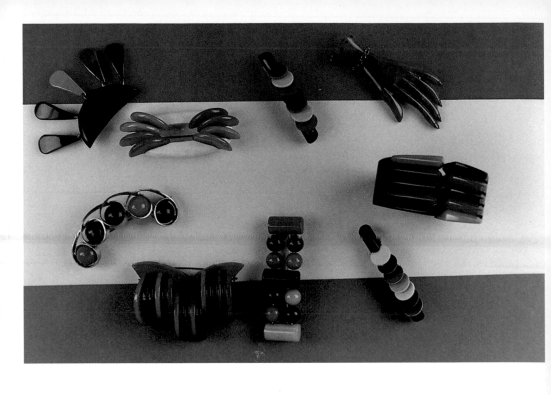

Opposite page:
Diverse group of Bakelite pins. (As Time Goes By). Top: $275-325, $275-325, $275-325, $375+; bottom: $175-225, $375+, $325-375, $275-325, $3000+

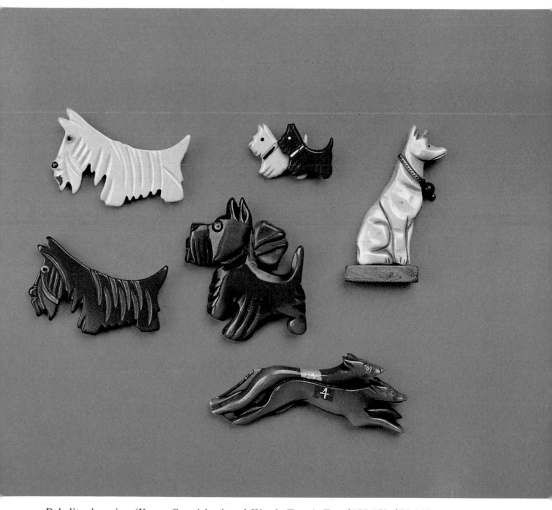

Bakelite dog pins. (Karen Carmichael and Wendy Tyson). Top: $125-150, $85-115; center: $135-165, $250-300, $135-165; bottom: $375-425

Opposite page:
Dog pin with wooden face and Lucite ears. Two similar Bakelite horse head pins. Wooden horse head with Lucite neck and mane. (Terry Rogers). Top: $100-145, $300-400; bottom: $275-375, $125-175

Celluloid dog, 1930s.
$50-60

Bakelite Scotty Dog pin. Painted collar and tongue, glass eyes, c. 1930. (Dennis Cogdell).
$150-175

Opposite page:
Plastic Scotty Dog with puppy attached by
metal chain. Pair of plastic Scotty Dogs
together in a pin. Small plastic dog pin.
(Linda Morgan). Top to bottom: $115-
135, $95-125, $115-135

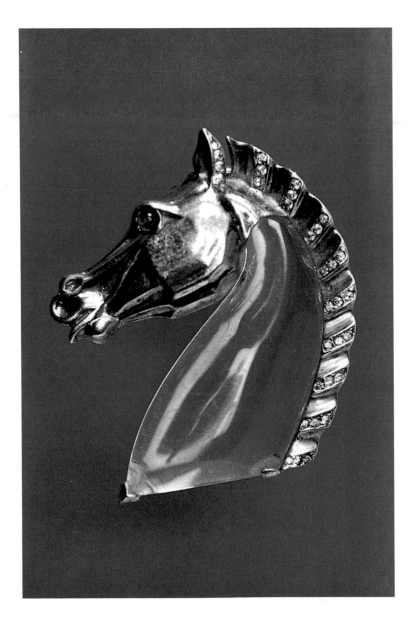

Trifari sterling and "clear belly" horse head and mane with rhinestones and colored glass eye. The name "clear belly" denotes the majority of the body in clear transparent plastic. (Karen Carmichael and Wendy Tyson). $450+

Signed *Trifari* salamander pin in clear belly style. (Angela Kramer Inc.). $450+

Assorted animal figurals in Bakelite. (As Time Goes By). Top: $250-300, $135-185, $125-150; center: $125-150, $175-225, $110-140; bottom: $125-150, $150-175, $175-225

Bakelite pins, necklace, earrings and bracelet all in horse motif. (Karen Carmichael and Wendy Tyson). Bracelet, top left: $200-250; Set, at top right: $175-200; horse pins: $300-475

Exotic animal pins. Turtle pin has green Bakelite shell and clear Lucite body. Giraffe and penguin pis are Bakelite. Bakelite owl pin. Lizard with transparent Bakelite body and sterling legs, head and tail. (Karen Carmichael and Wendy Tyson). Top: $175-225, $275-350; bottom: $195-235, $250-350, $195-275

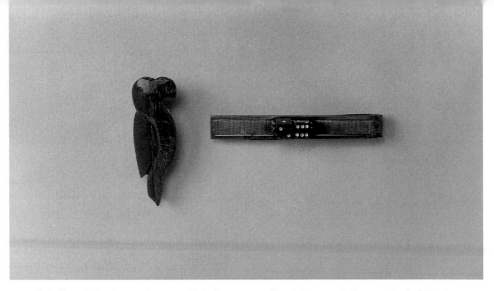

Bakelite pin in shape of parrots. Bakelite money clip with two red dice attached. (Wendy Tyson). L-R: $95-125, $75-125

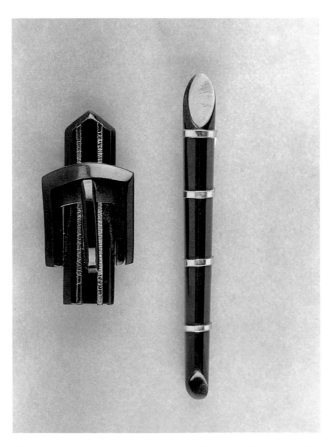

Plastic bar pin with chrome bands, Art Deco style. Brown buckle pin in plastic also with chrome decoration. (M. Klein). L-R: $85-125, $75-125

1950s brooch in plastic. Fox design in fuschia with hatched white pattern inside. Pin backing marked *Lea Stein*, Paris. (Linda Morgan). $150-225

Parrot head pin combining rhinestones for the head with red Bakelite
beak. Possible French origin. (Angela
Kramer, Inc.). $300-400

Plastic bird pins. (Jackie
Fleischmann). L-R: $100-135,
$85-115

Grouping of plastic bird pins. Red bird with black beak is a napkin ring made of Bakelite. (Terry Rogers). Top: $35-45; center: $75-120, $95-135; bottom: $85-115, $85-135

Clear Lucite animals, some with painted details, others with colored Lucite enhancement. (Karen Carmichael and Wendy Tyson). Top: $75-100, $75-100; center: $125-150, $95-135, $95-135, $75-100; bottom: $125-150, $125-150, $100-135

Examples of Bakelite in pins and earrings, c. 1930-1940. (Karen Carmichael and Wendy Tyson). Top: $175-225, $95-135 pr., $195-250; center: $275-350, $70-90 pr., $250-325; bottom: $175-250, $150-225, $95-110, $225-275

Yellow plastic parrot with blue rhinestone eye. Signed *Buch and Deichmann Copenhagen, Denmark.* (Wanda Johnson). $75-95

Assorted Lucite pins in animal, bird, fish and insect forms. (Karen Carmichael and Wendy Tyson). Top: $125-150, $100-125, $125-150; center: $150-175, $75-100; bottom: $100-125, $125-150, $125-150

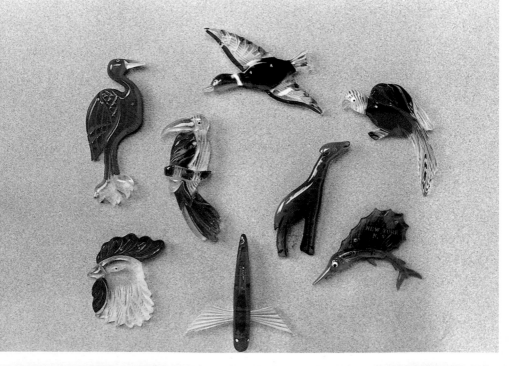

Green plastic frog with yellow metal backing. Peach colored plastic frogs also on yellow metal backing. Green plastic frog on ladder. (Linda Morgan). L-R: $175-225, $95-125 ea., $200-250

Plastic coral with faux pearls on gold filled hinged bracelet, signed *Miriam Haskell*. French fish pin with red and green crystal beads, faux pearls and plastic coral, marked *Dépose*. Plastic coral pin made in Austria. Gold filled wires entwine with light green crystals and dark green enamel leaves. (Muriel Karasik). Top to bottom: $300-400, $175-225, $150-200

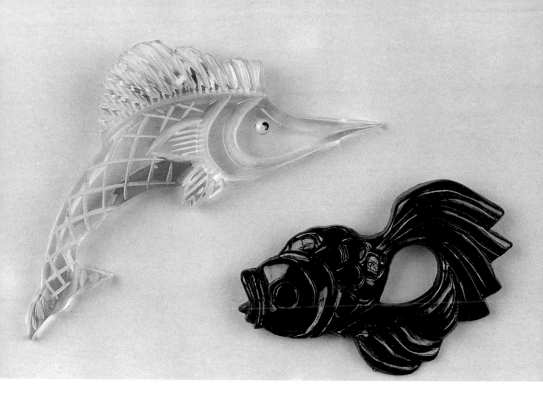

Black Bakelite fish pin. Transparent Lucite fish pin. (Terry Rogers). L-R: $125-150, $200-275

Bakelite and Lucite marine life pins, c. 1930-1940. (Karen Carmichael and Wendy Tyson). Clockwise (from pale yellow fish): $175-200, $400-500, $300-350, $125-175, $250-350, $175-200, $325-375, $115-145; center: orange fish, $300-375, orange shell, $100-135

Bakelite pins. (Mark Solomon). Top: $115-145, $135-155; center: $250-300; bottom: $125-175

Green translucent plastic cicada, c. 1920-1930. (Bizarre Bazaar). $200-250

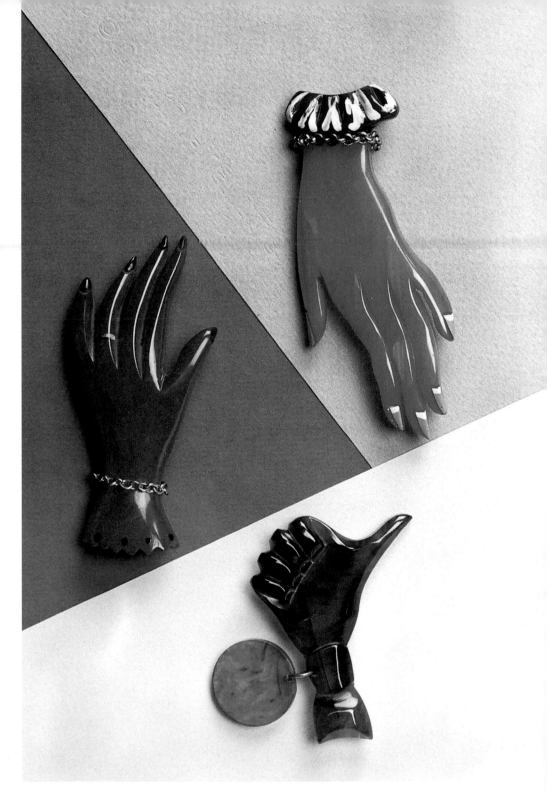

Three examples of Bakelite hand pins, design made popular by Co Co Chanel. (Wendy Tyson and Wanda Johnson). Top: $500+ ea.; bottom: $250+

Pins in the forms of people, faces and hands, all made from Bakelite. (Karen Carmichael and Wendy Tyson). Top: $250-350, $500+, $500+; bottom: $225-300, $550+

Child's crib toy in Bakelite. Painted eyes and held together on rawhide cord, c. 1930. (Dennis Cogdell). $250-300

1950s pin of Bakelite and straw in form of pumpkin character. (Angela Kramer, Inc.). $400-500\

Assortment of Celluloid pins. (Mark Solomon). Top: $65-95, $75-100; center: $65-85, $60-75; bottom: $60-75

Plastic pin in shape of Uncle Sam's hat. (M. Klein). $150-175

Plastic coffee pot charm. (M. Klein). $40-65

Celluloid *Popeye* with enamel colors. Layered plastic oval with female face. (M. Klein). L-R: $100-125, $70-90

Plastic football pin using metal chain attached at both ends to suspend plastic boot, megaphone and football helmet. (M. Klein). $400-500

Bakelite people pins most using plastic rings to create moveable joints. (As Time Goes By). Clockwise: $225-275, $650-750, $500+, $650+, $500-600, $600+; center: $600+

Plastic and Bakelite combined in pins and bracelet. (Karen Carmichael and Wendy Tyson).
L-R: $200-250, $400-450, $300-375

Layered Bakelite belt buckle and cuff bracelet. Ring with clear plastic setting, adorned with blue bead surrounded by rhinestones. Yellow plastic ring layered with black. Green marbled ring with yellow flat bead. Large red marbled plastic ring. (Muriel Karasik). Bracelet, $850+; buckle, $400+; rings, $100-150 ea.

Rings

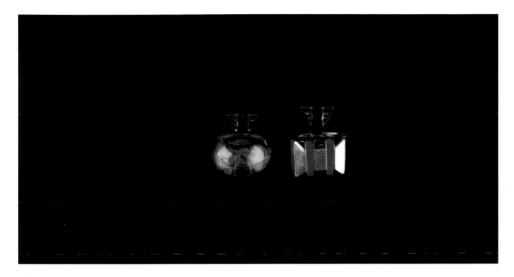

Three red fish enclosed within yellow Bakelite ring. Red enamel and metal ring, French. (Angela Kramer, Inc.). L-R: $200-250, $100-125

Black square ring layered with white plastic. Green translucent center shows (u of w) underneath on layered band. Red marbled rectangular ring. Yellow and tortoiseshell plastic ring. (M. Klein). Top to bottom: $100-125, $175-225, $70-95, $70-90

Bakelite rings. (Terry Rogers). Top: $65-95; center: $65-95, $65-95, $30-45; bottom: $45-60, $40-60

Bakelite rings sculpted and layered. (Karen Carmichael and Wendy Tyson). Top: $50-75, $55-80; bottom: $50-75, $60-75, $65-75

Men's celluloid rings made by an inmate at a North Carolina state prison probably fashioned from toothbrushes. (Scott Tyson). $150-200 ea.

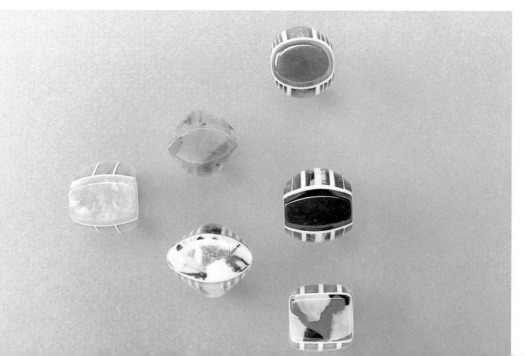

Groups

Plastic set of necklace pendant, pin and earrings, c. 1950. (Dennis Cogdell). Set, $125-150

Two butterfly pins with matching earrings. (Terry Rogers). Set, $175-225

Lucite pin and earring set, c. 1950. (Dennis Cogdell). Set, $75-100

Tinted and clear forms of Lucite jewelry. (Karen Carmichael and Wendy Tyson). Rings, $25-35 ea.; earrings; $25-35 pr.; bracelets, $65-125 ea.

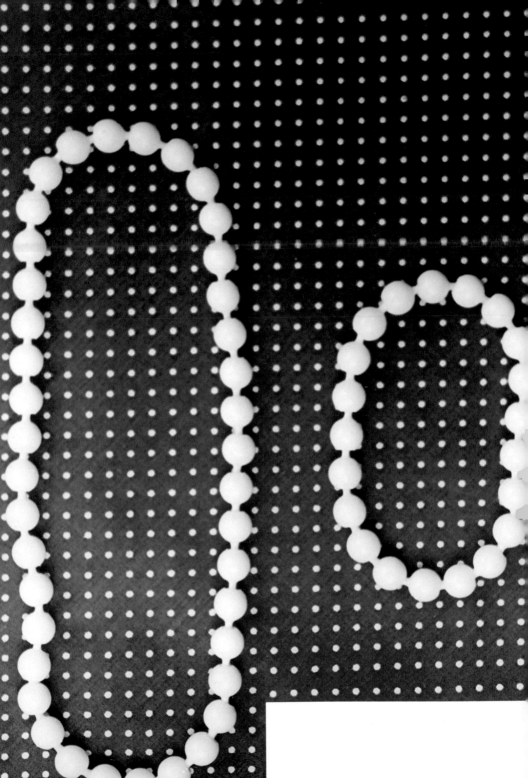

White pop-it beads made into a necklace and matching bracelet. (Matilda D. Knowles II). $10-20

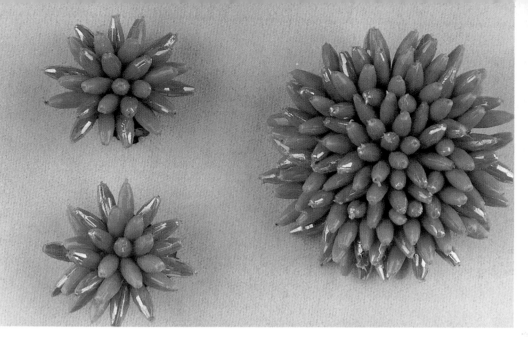

Set of pink plastic earrings and pin in chrysanthemum form. (Lorraine Matt). Set, $50-75

Bakelite set. Scotty Dog pin in black frame and matching Scotty Dog hinged bracelet. (As Time Goes By). $300-375 ea.

Black plastic and rhinestones in assorted forms. (Karen Carmichael). Heart pin, $50-65; celluloid box tie, $60-75; bakelite bracelet, $250-300; earrings, $50-60 pr.; bakelite necklace, $250-300

Opposite page:
The "Jackie" necklace by *Kenneth J. Lane.* This is a copy of an original, very elaborate necklace which was encrusted with emeralds, sapphires and rubies. It was given to Jacqueline Onassis by Aristotle Onassis and was later copied by Lane at her request. Lane was given permission to mass market the copies, some of which were done in plastic replicas of coral, turquoise and ivory. This example uses plastic cabochons, gold plated metal and rhinestones and includes matching earrings. Set, $1500-2000

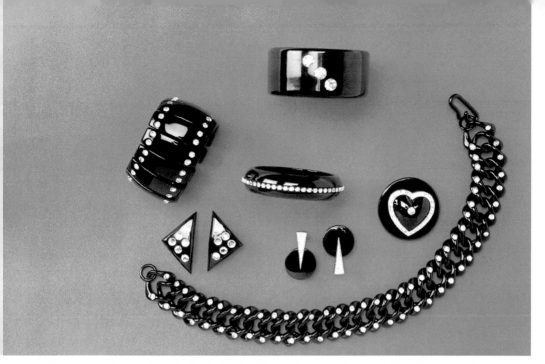

Rhinestone decorated black plastic, 1980s. (Karen Carmichael). Row 1: $75-100 (bracelet); row 2 (2 bracelets): $100-125, $50-75; row 3: $30-40 (earrings), $30-40 (earrings), $35-45 (pin); necklace, $70-95

Layered color in Bakelite pin, clip and pair of earrings. (Karen Carmichael and Wendy Tyson). Earrings, $200-300 pr.; pin and clip, $300-400 ea.

Opposite page:
Colored beads in various shapes and designs create pins and a bracelet. (Karen Carmichael and Wendy Tyson). Top: $350-450; bottom: $325-375, $225-275

Yellow and black cubed bracelet with matching pin. Both made from Bakelite. (Linda Morgan). Set, $400-500

Necklace of large green and yellow marbled square beads with wound wire spacers. Ring to match. Two green plastic carved rings. (As Time Goes By). Necklace, $175-225; matching ring, $50-65; Other rings, L-R: $50-65, $60-75

Bakelite polka dot sets. (Karen Carmichael and Wendy Tyson). Polka dot bracelets, $250-
350 ea.; earrings, $125-150 pr.; ring, $100-125; diamond bracelets, $1000+

Bakelite set with tortoise colored link chain from which hang brown and yellow sculpted drops. (As Time Goes By). L-R: $175-225, $150-200, $275-325

Buckles and Buttons

Brown translucent plastic belt. Two link bracelets with buckle motif, c. 1930. (Linda Morgan). Top: $195-245, $175-195; bottom: $200-250

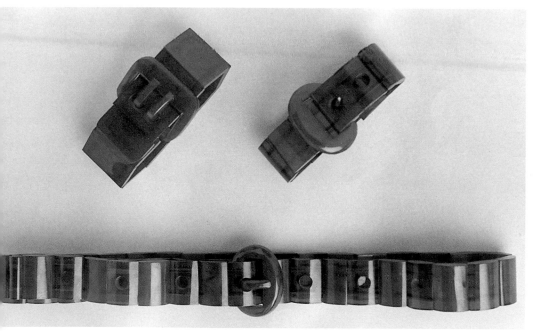

Opposite page:
Green and black Bakelite set with metal trim. Hinged bangle bracelet, earrings and dress clips. (Linda Morgan). Top: $150-200 pr.; bottom left: $450-550; bottom right: 75-100 pr.

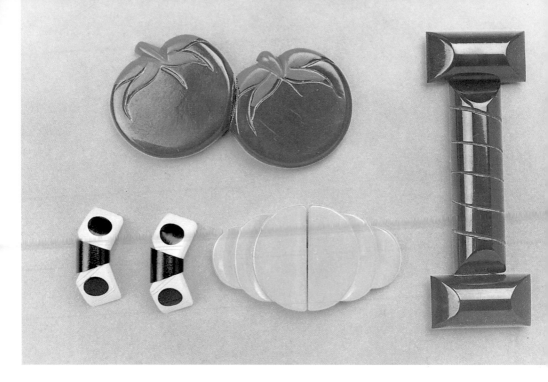

Three Bakelite belt buckles and set of clips. (Karen Carmichael and Wendy Tyson). Top: $200-275; bottom: $50-75 pr., $95-115, $165-185

Arrangement of bar pins and clips in Bakelite, c. 1930-1940. (Karen Carmichael and Wendy Tyson). Column #1, top to bottom: $70-95, $90-110; 2nd column: $100-125, $70-90; 3rd: $150-175, $95-125 pr., $95-125 pr., $175-200; 4th: $185-245, $70-95; 5th: $70-95, $125-175, $115-145; 6th: $80-120

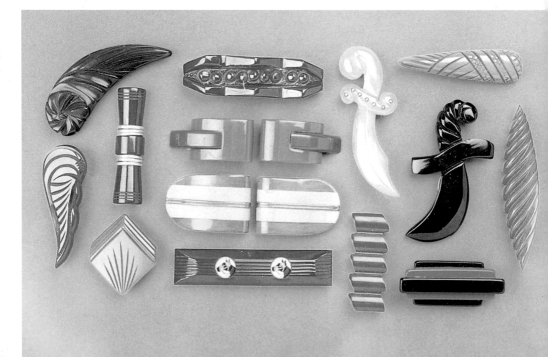

Plastic belt buckle with
ten matching buttons.
(Jackie Fleischmann). Set,
$200-250

Belt buckle with nine layers of color and matching clip. (Linda Morgan). L-R: $275-300, $325-400

Celluloid belt buckle from late 1920s. Fish form painted gold, red and black. (Smithsonian Institution). Special (?)

Plastic belt buckle elephants tugging a black ring. (Linda Morgan). $300-350

Bakelite belt buckle of black brick pattern background with white lizard, c. 1930. (Linda Morgan). $275-325

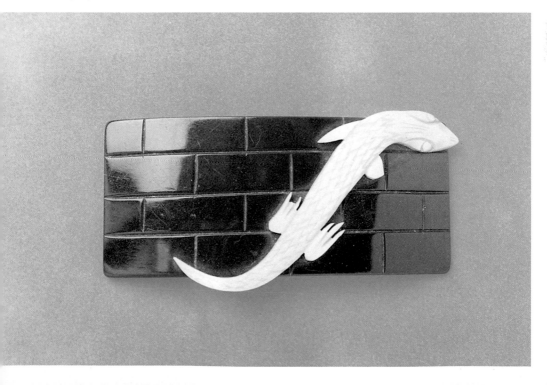

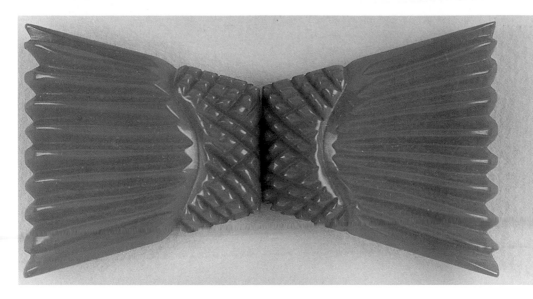

Amber bow shape Bakelite belt buckle. (As Time Goes By). $150-175

Brown and yellow Bakelite necklace on light brown plastic link chain. (Wendy Tyson). $195-250

Round marbled plastic belt buckle. Black and white belt buckle. Silver colored metal belt buckle and matching pin with cabochon style colored plastic stones. (M. Klein). Top: $125-150; bottom: $100-135, $110-135

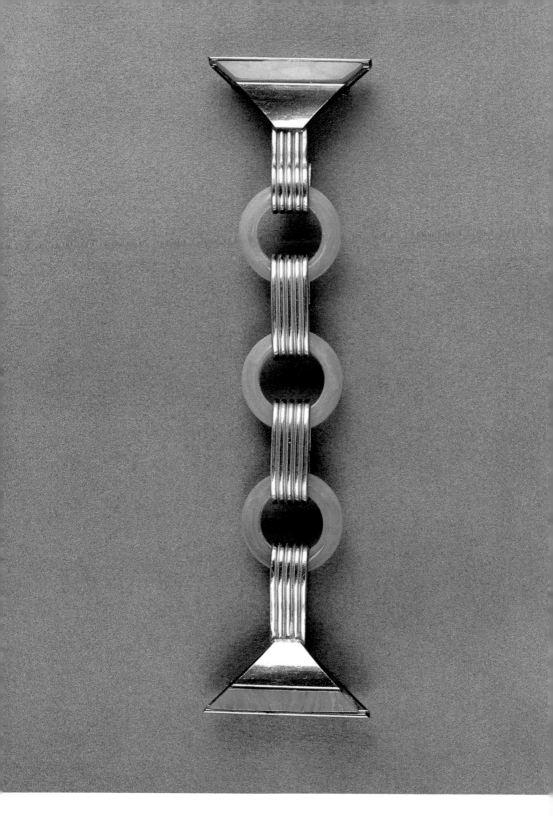

Yellow plastic and chrome linked belt buckle. (As Time Goes By). $150-175

Plastic belt buckles, two showing plastic mother-of-pearl accents. (M. Klein). $75-100 ea.

Plastic molded buttons. (Jackie Fleischmann). $50-65 ea.

Amber colored plastic belt buckles. (M. Klein). $120-145, $85-115

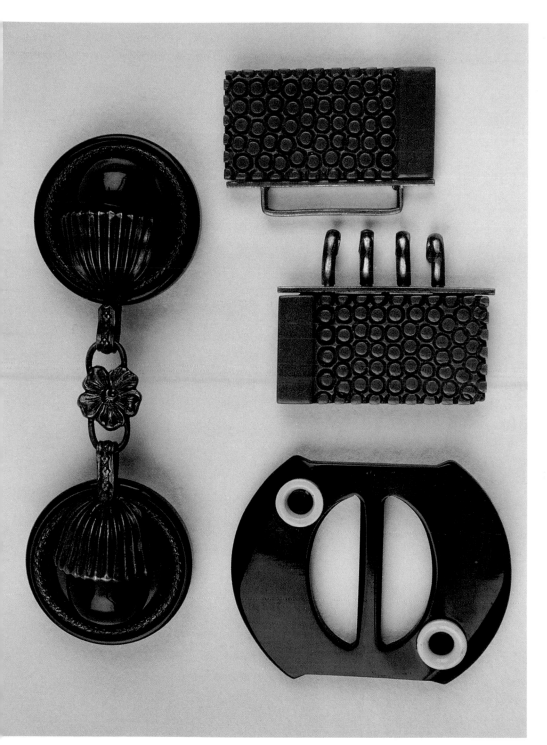

Group of Bakelite belt buckles. (Terry Rogers). Top: $70-95; bottom, $75-100, $50-75

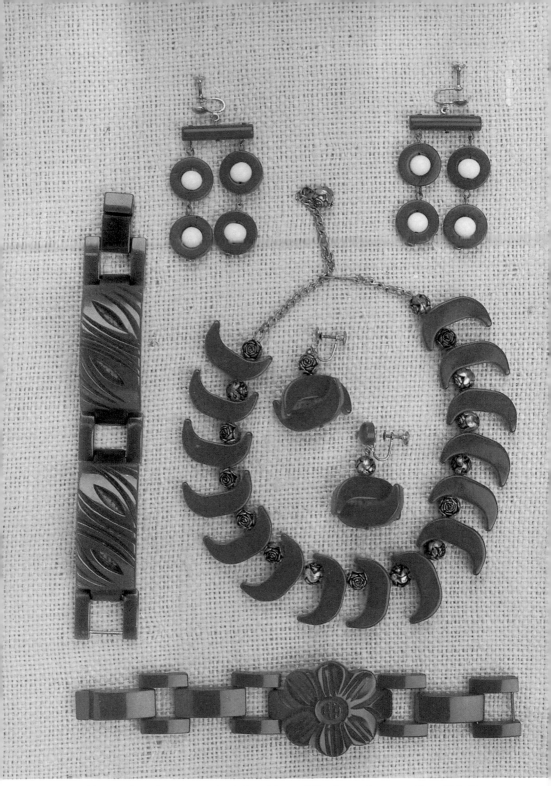

Necklace and earring set of red Bakelite with metal floral carved spacers. Green Bakelite link bracelet. Red and white dangle Bakelite earrings. Red linked bracelet in Bakelite with central floral accent. (Karen Carmichael and Wendy Tyson). Top: $85-115 pr.; center: $200-250, $300-400, set; bottom: $275-350

Plastic hair ornaments made in Japan. (Maureen McEvoy). $100-125 ea.

Amber colored plastic bug pin. Black bracelet with carved floral design and hinged back. Red crescent shaped pin and carved red plastic ring. Spider pin with red plastic body and metal legs. Black plastic sea horse pin. (Bizarre Bazaar). Top: $85-115, $250-300, $170-195, $85-100; bottom: $85-115, $200-250

Matching necklace and earrings with colored confetti suspended in clear Lucite. Lucite wrap bracelet and red Lucite pin. (Karen Carmichael). Set, top left: $100-135; bracelet, $85-120; pin, $40-50

Chrome and Bakelite necklaces. German origin. (As Time Goes By). Top (red): $225-275, $150-225; bottom (black): $150-225, $125-175

Bakelite pins and pair of earrings, early examples. (Ann's Arts). Top: $60-80, $50-75, $65-90; center: $100-125, $50-75; bottom: $45-65, $70-90

Bakelite and chrome. Bakelite seen here in amber, yellow and purple. (As Time Goes By). L-R: $165-185, $225-275, $175-250